LEAVING THE NARROW PLACE

Leaving the Narrow Place

Dorothy Field

OOLICHAN BOOKS

LANTZVILLE, BRITISH COLUMBIA, CANADA

2004

Library and Archives Canada Cataloguing in Publication

Field, Dorothy, 1944-

Leaving the narrow place / Dorothy Field.

Poems.

ISBN 0-88982-199-2

1. Jews—Poetry. I. Title.

PS8611.I34L42 2004   C811'.6   C2004-905152-0

The Canada Council | Le Conseil des Arts
for the Arts | du Canada

We gratefully acknowledge the support of the Canada Council for the Arts for our publishing program.

BRITISH
COLUMBIA
ARTS COUNCIL
Supported by the Province of British Columbia

Grateful acknowledgement is also made to the BC Ministry of Tourism, Small Business and Culture for their financial support.

We acknowledge the financial support of the Government of Canada through the Book Publishing Industry Development Program for our publishing activities.

Published by
Oolichan Books
P.O. Box 10, Lantzville
British Columbia, Canada
V0R 2H0

Printed in Canada

Contents

9 Leaving Mitzrayim

1 *É peregrino quiunque e fuori della sua patria.*
Anyone who has left home is a pilgrim.

13 Lost and Found
14 Orchard
15 After the Fall
16 To Tokeiji
17 Before Tokeiji
18 Hold Out
20 Confluence
21 The Last Hay
22 Haying with Ophelia
24 Sex Education
26 Lists
27 Fossils
28 Salad Days
29 There Was No Way
30 But in Her Own Way
31 1955, Harrison, New York
32 Ironing
34 P.S. This was before Eldridge Cleaver, Bobby Searles,
   and the raised Black fist
35 Black Velvet Bag
36 The Pillow
38 For Tenzin Gyatzo

2 *Perché il mar non ha paese nemmen' lui.*
  Because not even the sea has a home.

43 The Old Blue Dress
44 Haying with Saint Francis
46 Words with the Church
48 How to Praise
49 Elk
50 Haying with Hannah Senesh
52 Haying with Fanny
53 Desert Speak
54 New York, 1946
56 New York, 1946—My mother's side of the story
57 Haying with God
58 In the wind, in the sand and sage
59 What I haven't said:
60 What scared me, in no particular order:
61 (Trying to) Hay with My Grandmother
62 Speaking with My Mother
63 Green Gloves
64 Spanish Civil War: My Father's Choice
65 Music Box
66 Polish Guide
67 Not That It's So Much Easier
72 I, may I find home

3 *Love allows us to walk*
  in the sweet music of our particular heart.

75 Ruach
76 Mountains and Poetry—Helen Humphreys, Banff, 2003
77 Saskatchewan Tikkun
78 Ora et Labora
79 In the Brush by the Railroad Tracks or the Gully by the Stream
80 Danceland Saturday Night
82 Tomato Fugue
84 Calling
85 Southern mist and the ecumenical world is singing
86 Zimzum: Creation with Caribou
87 Haying with Gertrude and Alice
89 Haying

90 Scar
91 In the Throat Mountains
92 Khirkha, Palestinian woman's veil, silk cross-stitch
   on handspun linen, Museum for Textiles, Toronto
94 Challah
96 Fawn
97 Sunday Afternoon and Bach is Playing
98 There is a Moss
99 Let us praise the Garry Oak

4 *There are mountains hidden in mountains.*
There are mountains hidden in hiddenness.

103 Crossroads Poem
105 Haying with Groucho
107 Jew in the Abbey
109 Honey House
110 I will ask for birds
111 Haying with Murasaki Shikibu
113 Boxing Day Field
114 Burning Bush
115 Barred Owl
116 The blossoms are so brave
117 Goldstream Reprise
118 The Narrow Place
119 Pruning Wisteria
120 When time was food
121 Blessing
122 Haying with Death
123 How Does the Heart
124 Notes on the Text
127 Acknowledgments

Leaving *Mitzrayim*

I used to dream a cabin in a meadow, one room,
a table and chair, tiger lilies in spring, in fall
the shiver of dry grass. I'd pack my knapsack—

jar of green tea, bread, a chunk of cheese,
the small quilt I work before I go to sleep—
set out for meadow light, find myself

at dusk unable to follow blazes on the trees.
But every trail leads back—as if I didn't know.
There is no leaving

mitzrayim.

*

I could call it *mitzrayim*, the narrow place, could
call it the beast, conjure up her filthy coat, dirty nails,
shock you, then whine and cajole
for your sympathy—until I tire of my voice,
my strategies. The narrow place
is my own, the stories, the scars, the grief, all mine—
I am here once more, once more
sunk in an emptiness extending starless
beyond forever, again reaching
for courage, for the tenuous alchemy to bear the re-
membering.

If I could let my heart bleed—and I do—
if I could pick up my quilt—and I do—begin stitching
one stitch at a time, hands
moving, up and down, weeping,
binding layer to layer
myself to myself.
When I am all wept out, I wrap myself in my quilt,
and sleep.

*

Wake to shadows, those I'd left
or sought to leave behind, my family going
    back and back—
those who fled the kaiser, those who fled the czar
some with connections, some with only
    a landsman's address
the ones who peddled sewing thread and ladies' hose
the ones who garnered wealth and fame
the ones who wanted what they couldn't have
those who tried and failed
the ones who grew up coddled, the ones who were
    unseen
the ones who wanted not to be Jewish
the angry ones, the staunch ones, those who were
    wistful and dreamy
the ones who were brave and generous
the ones who were cheap and stinted their families
this family that hurt me as I hurt them, that tried their best as I
tried mine, that built their walls as I built mine, that called me
names as I named them, that took their revenge as I took mine,
were failed as I was failed, left as I was left, loved as
I was loved.

All of these stories are love stories.

1

É peregrino quiunque e fuori della sua patria.
Anyone who has left home is a pilgrim.

—Dante

Lost and Found

That year I studied loss.
On quiet days I'd visit the woods,
pockets where five kinds of orchid
used to bloom, places I'd avoided to

avoid the pain of absence. And there they were
renewed:
in April, rayed calypsos, stalks of spotted coral-root
fewer than before

but present.
July, I walked again.
The *habenaria* had not returned, nor the hooded ladies' tresses
but I found spiky blooms of rattlesnake plantain
above milk-veined leaves.

I almost lost
the loons
but I never lost their cries, bits of crystal
tossed against cedar walls, shattered to tears, and echoing,
        echoing
in the luminous grey.

Will-o-the-wisp, this study of loss,
phosphorescent minnows in a midnight sea.

The morning after leaves
nothing to hold
but a haze of memory, the dot-dot-dash
of light on eelgrass,
the neon dart of fish in black water,
        the ocean's green mind.

Orchard

Apples today, trees heavy with fruit,
ladder propped against a trunk,
wooden boxes filling, a ruddy man,
high wire angel, picking himself

home. The sky is buttered blue but shadows
hold the dark. Each fruit is green chill,
red chill, a weight
in an outstretched palm. He twists each umbilicus.
The stem releases—a silent snap of separation.
No past, no future, only one hand

reaching. We planted this orchard
thirty years ago, chose these
old varieties sometimes for their names alone:
Bramley's Seedling, King David,
looked for a Seek-No-Further—didn't find one.

Someday others will live here,
learn each tree's secret, the early pie apples,
the red that get sweet
only after frost, the green that keep
till spring. Hang a swing for their kids.
Or not.
                      Maybe they will raze
the shiplap farmhouse, build a
pink post-modern stucco with a three-car garage.

Today is only apples
breathing in the darkening air
breathing out the earth.

How we lose
our way   grow
homeless
   how the earth

that held us
sluices away
   rain and rain and rain
     the pond
overflows
      the bank where

muskrats tunneled
caves in
   nettles
     poke between
the slats of the bridge

thistles choke the apple trees

lichens cloak
their bark
green   grey   grey-green
     paint flakes
    off the barn's red door
jasmine pries loose
      roof shakes
   how we bundle

our scraps   hoist them
to our shoulders   go
   down the road

To Tokeiji

Swaddled in fog, I slide from my husband's house
flee to this narrow freedom

exposed now as the great bronze Buddha
who sits below, his back to the sea.
Rain washes his bent shoulders, puddles in his robe

Persimmon season I enter these gates
orange fruit strung to dry under wooden eaves
or still hanging like lanterns from bare branches

Here in the hills oak leaves, tarnished copper
spark the wind

Crows' caws
echo hollow across the tight valley

The abbess hands me a twig broom, I sweep
gingko leaves from stone paths, tend stone memorials
to abbesses past, tidy stone lanterns in the lichened graveyard

At night I dream of tides
When the gates close, I shave my head, take up robes
Now the stubble on my scalp grows grey

And the crows call
caw caw . . . haw, haw

There is no shelter
only learning to live
roofless

Before Tokeiji

Some days when
winds rock the bronze bell, memories rise

like wraiths: gloss of green *tatami*, our *kura*
full of silk scrolls, his grandfather's
haiku, porcelain cups

storage jars from Shigaraki, what was mine
never mine, my son's weight in my lap
wind soughing the pines, his cries

how I pulled him close, pulled closed
the outer shutters to secure our paper house

in its wooden skin, how I thought I would live there
forever

tend his family altar and their
graves, lead the ancestors
home for *Obon*

cook their favorite
foods, simmered eggplant, pickled
bracken, cold summer

noodles, set out lacquered plates, candles
in lanterns I made from worn shoji, how he turned

to a younger woman, how I kissed my sleeping son
wrapped myself in fog, slipped
away

Hold Out

Over my bed Christ hangs, a small copper form
on a tiny wooden cross
suspended from a picture hook, and I wonder

how I got here. Stretched below I sense Mary
in the fluorescent blue of my nylon blanket.
Where are the nuns who used to live here?

In my small cell
I am the Jew,
gristle
in the mouth of the Church, though this place is
full of us—in the words of the Psalms, stories of the Bible.
I am stranger
and guest
and more than stranger—
stiff-necked hold out,
one of the Chosen People.
Still here
staking my claim—
Children of Abraham,
my name, not yours.

My last morning, Brother Raymond reads from Jeremiah
stumbles on the Hebrew names, a text about Greeks and Jews,
the ones who wouldn't listen.
You are so peaceful
says Brother Anthony as I leave
    hands me two saints cards
                    Mary & Jesus
for remembrance, for return.

Inside, I am all knot
and cross-grain—
the beauty of the plainsong, the sting
of holy words, the discord
in your harmony.

Listen—
    I am listening, my footfalls on your stone floor.

Confluence

Six months ago I left Poland. My grandmother left
one hundred years before, driven out
by the czar. Lucky for her. Fifty years later she was
not burned at Auschwitz.

A Pole told me my grandmother's *shtetl*
was lovely—Ulanov—two hours
southeast from Krakow, the confluence
of two rivers, wildflowers

along the banks, wild birds, a place
she couldn't stay, a mark on the map
holding its ground despite shifting
borders, her starting point

to a new world, greenhorn child, piece work, sweat shops,
her husband a seller of ladies' lingerie, a life
not easy, but far
from Europe's slaughter. To me
she was an ear, a lap

a pair of hands. Last spring I returned, followed
her trail, full circle, but not
home, as alien as she was, no roots
left to search.

The Last Hay

Last summer's sweetness, I cut the baling twine,
bury my nose in hay, toss it
to the mules.

I didn't know then, June, that I was wayward,
thistle floss on wind, didn't know I was
groundless, chasm-bound.

I breathe this green honey, reverie and loss, the yearly
round, the much too much
of work.

My mother used to spray cologne on my wrists,
behind my ears, the scent atomized,
then gone.

    *

That last summer, fear's asp curled in my chest.
I startled to everything that moved.

When you said No More, you would live here
No More the black tar that stopped
my throat gave way.

I knew then I was grass beneath the blade.

Haying with Ophelia

Each year the blade shears the field
lets fall a golden thatch—
honey stripes curing on green stubble
the earth's sweet contours revealed

      Why do I think of Ophelia?
        skin unearthly white
        water-logged legs

heaps of fallen hay like skirts torn off

      Why do I think of myself
      green as spring?

        Tumble-down shack beyond the hedge
        my friend Stephie's back yard
        grimy windows
        glass jagged, missing
        rat-stench
        unzipped men, her father's
        cronies
        the rasp of their breath
        my terror
        crouched, elbows to ears
        don't look
        hear Stephie's cries
        nothing more

color bleeding from new mown hay

      Years later I looked for Stephie—she'd married a
      policeman, moved to Colorado
      swallowed bottles of pills.

I mouth my requiem for *mille-fleurs* tapestries of grass
bug-swum, snake-slithered, mouse-roamed—
think of Ophelia, of Stephie
and me—
wish us kids again and
whole, pockets full of
owl pellets, mouths ripe with jump rope rhymes
fingers dripping pokeberry juice
       our strong arms grasping the sisal string
       tossing bales off the wagon into the loft.

Sex Education

In her second installment, years after she'd
laid down the basic facts, my mother said—
in the bedroom with the door closed
in a low voice, avoiding my eyes
to make sure I knew
what was going on—
> *It's beautiful*
You don't have to have
> *penetration*
> *Would you like to see*
> *my diaphragm?*
> *Would you like to see*
> *a shrink?*

Didn't she know
I had another teacher?
That some nights my bedroom door opened
> very
> quietly
a crack of light etching the hardwood floor
a hand, two hands
at my shoulders
sliding along my skin, down
my spine, lower

was I awake
or asleep
> should I be
> should I
> > let him know
> > > not sure
> > > then
> > > or now
> > > > what it was
> > > > that touched me
> > > > down there

each glimpse a flashed
fragment

what to believe
my father said he'd prove me
wrong, take a lie detector test

I know
and cannot know
the slash of light on the floor
his body weight on my bed
how I planned my escape out my bedroom window onto the roof
the leap across to the pine's outstretched branch

The daytime father
writer editor storyteller
political know-it-all
the one who raged

The darktime father, the one with no words

The one who led me to language
The one who silenced me

Lists

What was taken:

The idea that family meant safety
A willingness to chance intoxication, all kinds
        to lose control
The insane invincibility of those who think
        they're young.
A belief in my strange beauty
        this Jewish nose
        this frizz of hair
        me, shining
My memory
Living in home skin

What was left:

A tendency to choke and gag
Skin, pores, cells steeped in mistrust
A talent for living like a snake in winter
        barely moving
         eyes alert, ears tuned
        hollow footfalls, a door cracking open
Always checking my escape route
Fear: blind corners bears cougars dark men
        walking alone   parking garages
        subway tunnels   bus stations at night
        sudden noises   spiders   lightning
Hiding, running

Wanting you to know me
Making sure you won't

Fossils

This morning, deer tracks in snow, a cool imprint
    of moonlight.
Now these fossils ranged on my table, volcanic

ash and mud scribed with sycamore, ginkgo,
    pseudo-sequoia.
You can see where leaves folded

on leaves, where a branch
broke. You can split them finer, reveal

redwood needles, horsetail stems, still
telling stories. My skin, too, holds records:

places I was held
tenderly, times touch burnt like dry ice,

branded. Like these fossil flakes, born of cataclysm
and tumult—limbs snapping

trees tumbling, crashing, carried in hot muck, rolling
over and over down molten hills.

Salad Days

Years later I ask my mother her memories
of Fanny. *I hardly know* she says *I was
so young, barely thirty-five.*
My mother never cooked—

the kitchen a place she passed through to tell Fanny
we'd have veal for dinner, to sit alone
at the round table, her lunch

always the same—bright green escarole
in a wooden bowl, blue cheese vinaigrette on top.
Men don't like blue cheese, she'd say

banished it from family meals to save my father
distress. In her room behind the kitchen Fanny would knit
through my mother's lunch, till my mother settled

into a stuffed chair in the living room, the one
my father assumed after work.
She'd flip through *The New Yorker*, drift

her mind to games for my brother's
birthday, clown puppets to model with his boy scout troop
papier maché mountains

for their Lionel trains. In the kitchen Fanny would slip on
her apron, put just-delivered lamb chops
in the icebox, chop walnuts for *schnecken*, set the dough

to rise. To us Fanny wasn't hired help, more like
a grandmother—Fanny's old hands
the kindest machines as she

shelled limas, put potatoes to bake
prepared to feed us.

There Was No Way

my mother could have learned to cook
not as a child banished from the kitchen
where the cook held her upside down, spanked her

if she came in for company—
not later, with Fanny cooking magnificent
meals and between-meal snacks with no obvious effort.

Not that she didn't try.
In her earliest married days she found a recipe
calling for breadcrumbs, tore each shred and morsel

of dried crust by hand. No one
fed my mother, though there was
plenty of food and she ate, of course.

When she was sick her grandmother sent her
chauffeur to deliver roast squab under glass.
No one let her stir the batter. No one
sat with her in the kitchen

while she snacked on toasted almonds after school.
She never cooked for herself or me.
It was Fanny who taught me to roll out cookie dough

let me lick the bowl.
My mother was sent to learn other things—
how to paint watercolors, dabble in oils.

She taught me to copper enamel
sent me to learn pottery, a design class,
bought huge sheets of metallic foil in every luminous color

so we could sit with scissors and glue making cut out angels
for Christmas decorations, but that's another story.

But in Her Own Way

My mother fed me:

lunches at Benny's, shrimp salad on toast, while I twirled myself on the slippery stool at the counter, watching Benny make milkshakes, his magician-green blender, the long shiny shaft with the propeller on the end, foaming ice cream and milk, the sweat on the cold metal container, my contentment after I'd finished two tall glasses of chocolate manna.

Hamburger Heaven, straight-backed wooden benches with strong solid arms like gothic pews, the fattest patties, medium rare and dripping, reclining on their pillow-y buns, the huge white napkins we tied round our necks to channel the rivers of ketchup, raw onions, and relish cascading from earnest mouths.

Or at the Bird Cage, a ladies' retreat in the bowels of Lord & Taylor's, seats with one embracing arm that folded round to become a table. Dutifully I ate the main course, waiting rapt for the waitress—nurse-like in starched apron and cap—wheeling the stainless steel dessert cart with its three extravagant layers: glazed raspberry tarts, napoleons, maraschino cherries, thick mocha icing, rosettes of whipped cream, and me caught in the exquisite agony of choice.

1955, Harrison, New York

Epaminanas, what you got there?
Butter, Mammy.
Butter! That ain' no way to carry butter.

> The melting butter yellows Epaminanas' brown legs.
> Miss Angemeier, the school librarian, perches
> on her desk, a fox sparrow, mossy fawn and grey
> delivering her only story.
> It is the day before Thanksgiving, Christmas, Easter,
> the school a straitjacket strained at the seams.
> Miss Angemeier is coy. We have to coax her to begin.

When your Auntie give you butter
you wrap it in leaves, take it to the creek and cool it and cool it
and carry it carefully home.
You hear me, Epaminanas?

Yes, Mammy.

> The story snares us. By sixth grade
> we can say the words along with Miss Angemeier.
> His aunt gives Epaminanas a puppy. He holds it
> under water, as if it were butter. It nearly drowns.
> When she gives him a loaf of bread, hot from the oven,
> he ties a cord round it, leads it home
> like a puppy, arrives with a string of crumbs.

> Four times a year we rise like yeast
> to Miss Angemeier's fake drawl
> and the miracle—butter to puppy to bread,
> indulge our pleasure at another child's stupidity
> too sheltered to know that elsewhere
> other stories are being told.

You hear me, Epaminanas?
You hear me, Rocco?
You hear me, Hymie?

Ironing

What is spoken is by that speaking made to exist.
—Jane Hirschfield

My mother sends the sheets to the cleaners.
Milly irons the rest.

I stand in the back room watching
Milly, her arms moving, wrinkles
smoothing, sniff the damp of the sprinkled
laundry, her odor, clean and strange, wonder
why she doesn't smell like us—

the surprise of her pale palms
when everywhere else she is dark.

My great-great-grandfather owned slaves in Alabama—
started as a peddler with a mule, ended up a
cotton broker—only two, but enough to make me
wonder. Did he sit with his family round a *seder* table,
read the injunction:

Remember, we were slaves in Egypt

Milly doesn't rush, just keeps her arms moving, pulling
another damp shirt from the basket, laying it out on the
ironing board. I memorize the order—yoke, collar,
first cuff and sleeve, second cuff and sleeve,
buttonhole strip, the body of the shirt: side   back   side.
She fills the wicker basket—clean laundry, smelling of
sunshine, folded like a stack of books—leaves

at the end of the day. My mother drives Milly or sends her
by taxi, past the Barry Avenue store, home to
her own kids. After Milly there is Mamie, then Lee Pearl McCoy—
Mamie doesn't last long, her rage too close to the surface.
Some do cleaning, some cook and serve meals. At dinner

if I mention freedom marches, lunch counter sit-ins, a look
from my mother silences me—sssshhhh, it says, if we don't
say anything
maybe the women who do our work won't notice
they're Black.

P.S. This was before Eldridge Cleaver, Bobby Searles, and the raised Black fist

Don't get me wrong, my mother cared about the Black women who worked for us, still "Negroes" then, listened to their stories— how they tucked their money into secret places, scared of being mugged on their way back to Harlem, how they missed the warmth of the South, their resignation when their daughters got pregnant, no husbands in sight—

another generation for them to carry. There was no talk of *svartzes* in my house, no racial slurs of any kind, except my mother's grandmother calling my father *The Kike*—it didn't mean much, she said, just the way her crowd of German Jews talked about those Russian greenhorns. My parents voted Democrat, sent money to the NAACP, traveled abroad, lived in their small world: The Egghead Underground, with other M.O.T., as my father used to say.

Talking race with her cleaning women (or mentioning the class war within her marriage to anyone) would have offended my mother's tact and delicacy. The maids' blackness left them invisible. From their need, they shared their troubles with my mother. She listened, sheltered her own behind her curtain of privilege.

Maids came and went. The stories repeated themselves. My mother was no Molly Goldberg, no Mrs. Portnoy, would have been horrified if anyone imagined her feeding and nagging and feeding and nagging: *Eat, dahlingk, a little more kishke.* She bundled our old clothes for the Black women, bundled the women themselves into packages she didn't probe, their suffering just another thing else she could do nothing about.

Black Velvet Bag

                      Just yesterday I came across
this bag, still elegant, with its metallic rosette, survivor
from another time. In those days, all I needed were a few
bills, a pair of opera glasses. Then Jules died and I moved
across the park, a bank of windows over the avenue
and the pond beyond—winters
I could watch them skate.
                              Lovely, those rooms,
all mahogany, sterling and crystal, meals downstairs
in the oak dining room. By the time they knew
I was Jewish, the lease was already signed.

                          The gold thread
on the handle is a bit tarnished now. When did I find
time to stitch it? While Jules was alive there was so
much to do—opera, theatre, dinner with sisters, brothers,
their children, finding husbands for the girls, keeping
after the help.
                       And then the war—the fear
for those still in Germany, the grief: Polly lost,
then Evelyn, Ruth so timid she trembled
if you looked at her.
                          Now I find solace
in the garden—comfort in the feel of my hands in
cool soil. I'd like you to have the bag as a
keepsake, a relic from my time before.

The Pillow

When fever took my mother, barely forty,
(a few years later penicillin would have cured her)
everything with her name came to me.
For years I kept this pillow
made for her by her husband's mother
(my mother came unmothered to marriage
though her mother lived just up the park)
her initials D E M pricked in mesh,
lawn edged in lace, seams hand-rolled.
The stitches whispered welcome.

Small consolation, this booty.
We were starvelings, she and I.

With us, my mother was contained as bone
china, spent her days away talking
books and gossip, anywhere but home.
Her charm chilled me.
(except summers, sunlit pines above the eye
of the lake, feeding on doeskin, the rise of fish,
smell of balsam—always at the back of my mind,
the train back to the city)
I wasn't clever enough to hold her.

Winter afternoons, shadow brocaded the sofa,
fireplace cooled to ash. I stalked the elevator
watching its lights. If it slowed, my mother might emerge.
With her death, I stopped waiting.

I don't know why I remember
that kosher rule: "Thou shalt not seethe the kid
in its mother's milk." How not to,
I wonder. Children drink
or go hungry at their mother's breast.

Now I strip cupboards, pass this pillow and the rest
of my mother's things to my daughter.
Let her shoulder the grief.

For Tenzin Gyatzo

I. From his window in the Norbulingka
    the Dalai Lama saw willow   juniper   pines
    hung with giant cones
    wisps of clouds on a cerulean ground
    and beyond
    ring upon ring of mountains
    making his bed a tiny bark in a dryland sea

II. The Dalai Lama's ceiling was lemon yellow wattle
    dashed with citrus-orange beams
    lotuses blue blue-grey dusky sienna—
    perched between turquoise lintels on a cinnabar ground
    color fragrant as butter tea

III. Streams of nomads
     hair matted   ripe with grease
     prostrate themselves
     before the Dalai Lama's empty bed

IV. A Lhasa professor remembers his years
    in prison, nods to the secret Dalai Lama
    photo on his altar, sells carpets
    to visiting foreigners. In the kitchen
    his wife makes *chang* for locals

V. In the Tsurphu hills a yakman
    folds the blankets that cushion
    the pack saddles, touches the forbidden photo
    to his forehead, slides it between
    the flap of his red wool coat
    and his muslin shirt

VI. In Shigatse a silversmith
set a turquoise stone in a *repoussé* bowl,
glances up at the photo resting
between his workbench tools

VII. Absence so potent
it is presence

2

Perché il mar non ha paese nemmen' lui.
Because not even the sea has a home.

—Giovanni Verga

The Old Blue Dress

Faded, shoulders and back, its blue leached into the ravenous sky. Days I knelt, weeding, picking. The front still bright, blurred roses stretching pale leaves on thornless stems. I remember how we'd glory in the lines of seedlings, green shrill poking up from red earth. Watch them shrivel. So little beyond chores, tending chickens, pigs, children. I patched new patches over old, stitched stitches over stitches, some neat, some wild—when the clouds formed, promised, then moved on. One breast pocket—there used to be two—still holds a trace of clay, run with rickrack, furrows under the plow. Hunger maps. And Jake, slumped on the porch, big hands, swollen knuckles limp between his legs, wondering should we plant again or move. Then there was nothing left. Why did I keep this old dress, tending bad times like they were sons and daughters?

Beauty there, before the dust, morning mist, the fields spread, trusting as a bride, the sun a shimmer of red spending itself in the rusty soil. And Jake, as if I didn't know:

Looks nice don't make a living.

Haying with Saint Francis

Here in Saskatchewan the brothers wear small wooden crosses
shaped like a bird—an eagle? a dove?—wings spread to dry
or shelter us.

Our first day, Brother Dominic tells us about a young buck
too friendly for his own good, lovely furred antlers.
Don't feed him, Dominic says.
Hunting season is almost here,
the deer's chestnut coat the color these brothers would wear
if they wore robes.
St. Francis would have called him *Frate cervo*, Brother deer,
fed him from his open palm

                    or that's how Giotto painted him.
Walking over the fields
through thickets of saskatoons and choke cherry
I see him, Saint Francis, thigh high in prairie grass
scythe in hand swinging his arms as wind harries the meadow
cutting a path just wide enough for one
or maybe two
to walk these soft hills, hardly disturbing
badgers, fieldmice, crickets.

I remember that first meeting in the pink hills
of Assisi, when I read his canticle to the creatures,
met his family.
In this prairie valley I meet them again:
Frate vento, Brother wind—
        he has been here this week, churning
        the bleached heads of grass, running them in circles—

and *Sora aqua*, Sister water—she too,
        a horizontal rain that sent grasshoppers sodden for shelter
        flooded the poetry on my windowsill—

woke at midnight to stand with *Sora nostra matre terra*,
Our sister mother earth
> as the sky turned a pulsing silver tide
> and through the haze a pinprick of stars.

In a New Mexican village tucked above the Rio Grande, I bought a figure of St. Francis, head cocked, one arm stretched, a tiny sparrow perched at his neck, carved from elk antler by a man whose forebears came from Spain. He'd stretched canvas when he was young, for Georgia O'Keeffe, told me he was a Jew, how his people fled the Inquisition following Columbus.

Each year I place that elk Saint Francis on the *seder* table
when we retell the story of our people
leaving *mitzrayim*, wandering the desert
trying to find home.

The path unfolds under the scythe,
hugs the round of the hill as a collie hunkers after sheep
or a cat slinks low stalking birds

and I call on you, St. Francis,
with your tenderness for small beings,
walk me through these fields
shelter me, help me wrestle paradox—
Sister hawk, Brother vole.

Words with the Church

I sit among you, Brothers of Saint Francis,
morning prayers, 11 o'clock mass, weep to find myself
your sister, the disowned branch of the family—
the falsely accused, the wrongly convicted,
weep to see you there with the booty
even as I remember: How you called me names,
hunted me down, yet the kinship is there
within the feud.

Here in this Saskatchewan chapel I meet the Church, my
mother, the hidden Jew:

> like the *anousim* of Santa Fe, Albuquerque, Socorro, remem-
> bering Friday nights, their mothers drawing the curtains,
> lighting candles, holding their palms to shield their eyes,
> their father placing his hand on their heads to bless them,
> in September their grandfather roasting pork, then throwing
> it away secretly so the neighbors wouldn't know they were
> fasting.

Among you I find my likeness and my rage:

> The altar set like a *seder* table, unleavened bread, red wine.
> The priest raising the Bible, kissing it—though he stops short
> of our excess, the way we unroll the Torah scroll, use a silver
> pointer to avoid desecrating scribed letters, dress it in em-
> broidered satin, silver finials, parade it around the pews so
> we can touch it with extended prayer books—holding up
> the circle of the host (this morning the sun shone right
> through it turning it into a tiny glowing planet), breaking it
> carefully into even pieces, like the middle matzoh, though
> his flock swallows the pieces, doesn't hide half for the kids
> to hold for ransom, then put back together, a crumbly jigsaw
> puzzle.

How you made us carry the shame and darkness
you wouldn't bear.

I follow along in the prayer book, aware of the Brothers' questions:
Who is she, here every day, never going up for communion?
After prayers I ask a Brother for the number of the psalm he'd just read:

That's a good one, number 42. Some of them are hard,
full of patriarchal language, pretty militaristic . . .

A gentle man, this Brother, generous, undeserving
of my anger. And if not him, who?
And what shall I do with my grief?

I open the text, find the words:
I have no food but tears

To myself I say:

My tears are food and healing water,
Mirame attento, soy tu alimen—

Look at me carefully, I am your food.

How to Praise

*If a little dreaming is dangerous, the cure for it is not to
dream less but to dream more, to dream all the time.*

—Proust

                    I am planting
fall crocuses, an antidote
to the stab of their beauty. They make lavender
the color of mourning, appear

                    from nowhere
with the cicadas' first keening, rest stops
for wasps drunk on windfalls, their petals pearled
like abalone or the skin behind my ear.

Can I forgive them,
harbingers of moist darkness
                    and silence?

                    They lie
hidden, rise leafless from spent soil, poisonous
in all their parts. Meadow Saffron, their pale
stems remember

seasons underground.
Their beauty
                    the beauty of endings,

leading us
into false summer,
                    the ghosting frost.
                    I will plant them
everywhere, like fairy lights, in pockets below
the dogwood, beside the woodshed, the entrance
to the root cellar.

Elk

You'd like to be the novice of a deer.
You'd do whatever it told you.

—Tim Lilburn

Steam plumes from the elk's nostrils,
paired clouds lost to cold air.
The elk stands still.
Closer, I might see the moisture on his nose, the grooves
on his huge rack, nine points, maybe more—

But there are no elk, have never been elk, in these
domesticated
woods, this edged forest.

Still he stands, showing himself. I meet him
huge in the space between us. I might fall
to my knees but I am afraid
to open the car door.

I haven't always known to look.
First morning in Tokyo, Fuji's silver cone
filling my hotel window.
So easy, I didn't stop. It never came out
                                                  again.

I let the elk fill me. He shifts his golden rump, turns
into the woods. Leaving me
        my shopping list
        the rest of my day
        leaving me
        to myself
        this presence of elk
        living close
to his skin.

Haying with Hannah Senesh

I pray these things never end:
the sand and the sea, the rush of the water,
the crash of the heavens
                    —Hannah Senesh

Haying isn't heroic—not like you, Hannah. I thought of you
this morning, dew still on the grass—we'll cut later
once it dries—wished I could have you at my side, hear
your story in your own voice: how you woke
to streets rubbled in glass, all innocence

shattered—seventeen years old, my god, at seventeen
I barely knew my name—how you left for Palestine,
then parachuted in behind enemy lines, into Hungary,
the mouth of the beast, trying to save Jews in the camps,

when you could have stayed put, harvesting oranges
building the land, might have been there to receive
the broken ones after the war.

Haying stumbles, not like you, Hannah:
every year it's something—grass felled, then it rains
the bailer breaks, mules balk—and still

                              the epic of hay.
Do I sound too poetic? The largesse feels mythic,
this fragrant cache that fills the barn, carries us
through the dark—tidal as breath—
an upswell, a falling,
          a tossing on the earth's deep bed.

It's what you dreamed, Hannah, a life
tending the land, an unbroken cycle of seeds
and new-hatched chicks, not like
your life, all trajectory—two points
and the arc between

severed. In another life I would hay with you, Hannah.
You would drive the mower, slowly
stopping to praise
    each grasshopper
    each baby rabbit.

I would walk beside you, pitchfork
in hand, tidying windrows
    blessing new grass.

Haying with Fanny

Fanny stays close to the kitchen, her simmering
chicken soup, her counter veiled in noodle dough.
What would her parents make of this land where
even a Jew can own a stretch of fields,
a stand of fir? She pulls mint

from the ditch, steeps it for the tea we drink
when we return from the fields. Fanny remembers
haying from her childhood *shtetl,* the Poles,
their thick bodies swinging scythes,
stooking the hay into hummocks, sweat

darkening the horses' shoulders. Fanny's parents kept
geese in a dusty shed by the backdoor. She helped them
pluck down for feather beds, remembers the crawl of
chicken lice on her young body.

Goyische memories, and fearsome, this June haying—
bringing back the Easter pogroms, her family hiding
in the cellar, the peasants' rampage, brides
ravaged on their way to their weddings.

She puts out a plate of *schnecken,* cherry
preserves, familiar food, harvest fare, how she
mothers our bodies.

Desert Speak

Listen: the desert speaks salt, speaks
resin of mesquite and creosote,
flick of a salamander tail, palimpsest
of bird track over snake trail,
a language all

liquid and its lack—
the keyhole in pink rock
where a spring rises, sometimes,
its course marked by desert holly
in sluiced sand, the roar of flash floods,

now silence. See how water
cut the chasm between those silty rocks, how
it swept through this *wadi* into each frail
crevice. See

how the salt bush
spreads cilia roots to suck iotas of water
and the *ocotillos*, spare skeletons of thorn, stretch red
tongues to rain.

New York, 1946

The painting over my mother's desk is dark—
blues and greens and blacks—
except for yellow streetlights.
My mother doesn't sit at her desk. She lies
on a chaise under an afghan. I cannot see her face.

I am hungry. If I go to the kitchen
Fanny will give me something to eat.

I stand in the doorway,
cannot move.

I want her to see me
so I know I am
still here.

The sky is black though it could be any time of day.
I try to be like her, still and empty and very far away.

Annotations to New York, 1946

1. This is not the memory I planned to write. I hoped to recall
   the Washington Bridge lit at night, the view from our apartment
   across to the Palisades, the exultation of V.E.Day. This memory
   freezes out all the others.

2. Fanny was my father's cousin, same age as my grandmother.
   She cooked for us. Delicious food.

3. My parents started marriage in twin beds. After a trip to France
   they switched to one large one, its curved blond headboard
   matched the curved-front bureaus. My mother went to bed
   early, sat up reading, eating thin-sliced scallions on buttered
   bread.

4. I see the room as if through scrim, all color seeped away, except my mother's chaise, blue-green, and her heather afghan.

5. In my first draft I wrote, "I am held/ in the doorway" though I wasn't held at all.

6. My mother lay as if felled. Her father dead of a heart attack. In his fifties. We lived in the city then.

7. This memory is impossible. It takes place in the suburbs, where we moved a year later.

8. The poem is tight, words like currency in a miser's fist. This is the lie. In my mind the space stretches beyond comprehension.

9. I had thought this was *my* childhood I remembered. Today, I realize it is hers. She gave me her loneliness, the thing she truly knew, and her grief.

10. I regret the narrowness of my sympathy.

New York, 1946—My mother's side of the story

She thinks I don't see her, there
in the doorway, small, tentative,
tenacious. If I just lie still, maybe she will go away.
How did I end up in this huge
house—
lawns, perennial borders, acres of woods? Twelve rooms.
When friends ask, I lie, say there are only eight,
don't mention the five bathrooms. I pictured an
apartment on Riverside Drive, afternoons in the park while
the kids rode the swings, lunches at Schrafft's.

A year ago I thought I might go
home, to the city, to my father—if I'd known what to do
with the kids. My father was
past all that. Nothing now
but get used to the rage—this walking landmine
of a husband—my father so gentle, never raised
his voice—dead so young,
when I still needed him.

If I just lie here she will go
to the kitchen. Fanny will
feed her. Why does she stand
staring, fixed, as if I might
disappear?
Crazy, this idea of refuge—
as if my father, remarried to a woman who could think of
nothing but tennis, would have wanted me. He told me
I wasn't sexy enough—sexy enough for what
I wonder.
Shipwrecked,
on an aqua chaise, alone with this Russian madman, hot
red hair, cold green eyes.

Still there, in the doorway, waiting—
small, tenacious—
the other half of my own loss.

Haying with God

when I say god
        whose god/who's god
  when I say god
        small one, me
               left
    when I say god
        cold breath, bleak night

    When
            afraid / left
      I say
            here in silence

        when I say
            no end to

      god
            dark   *don't let me be*

      when I say god

             al(l)one

In the wind, in the sand and sage

in that color that is
no color, that is rain bleaching tone
turning spring's first flush

into dust and tumbleweed and racing clouds
brushing the bluff where Susan hoped to lie.
When she said that, we couldn't imagine her death

so soon
buried across the continent—
marble gravestone, sturdy gate, closely fenced plot

where the green hurts your eyes.
I have a quilt cover she pieced by hand, running stitch
triangle patterns of kitchen yellows

boat blues. After she died I sewed another
laid it over Susan's, laid filling between
stitched them together.

Because I wanted her
to hold me. Because I hadn't heard enough
of her licorice dreams, dark and sweet and salt.

Because I wanted for us a looser home
that faded denim sky
land naked as a promise.

What I haven't said:

How Susan died, on a summer night, of an overdose
in an unfinished house
after a sojourn in the psych ward.

How my brother, her husband
who loved her
for her blond hair, her poetry

her extravagant wit, panicked
at despair: *Get well*
or else.

How she chose, or had no choice,
how in death he longed to own her
Susan wife of David, his words on her stone.

Abandoned his grief—
Keep moving, my mother advised.
How he got cancer after marrying a
second blond,

then married again, a third time
to a second Susan,
his death before

he turned forty.
How he gave me
her quilt top, the only thing I have of her.

What scared me, in no particular order:

My parents on the lawn with friends singing to a Les Paul guitar, someone mentions McCarthy—the grown-ups all get silent / Black and white TV, footage of bulldozers shoving piles of corpses, starved, naked, hardly bodies at all, you can see the bones inside the skin, the machine rolling them over and over, arms shooting out, folded back into the pile. Kindergarten, holding out my hands for inspection, nails dirty, Mrs. Gasparini makes me stay on the bench by the wall, I can't move to the tables in the center with the other kids / My parents refusing to take the loyalty oath. What's a loyalty oath? / My older brother home from The House of Wax, a 3-D movie with weird cellophane glasses, so frightened he moves from his own room back to the extra twin bed in mine / Me outside my older brother's door overhearing my father explain to him about abortion, clothes hangers, butchers / Friend of my parents runs for the local school board, McCarthy-style slander, his career ruined / That I'll never be able to stop sucking my thumb, like my older brother who sits reading, two thumbs in his mouth, his first fingers stroking his nose / Supervisor of schools, Joe Vassallo, juicy man with a round red face, one of his clients goes mad, bites off the tip of his nose, they sew it back on—you can see the scar, the line of stitching / Sent to my room, someone comes to check on me, I scream: GO AWAY. They do / TV screen again, News Bulletin: Joseph McCarthy Dead Today—screen goes black / My father home from work, goes into the back room with my mother, shuts the door, angry sounds, muffled voices—I wait for them to come out, tell us they're getting divorced / I'm caught with my best friend cheating on a music exam, sent to the principal, none of us able to believe it—we're the brains, the good girls, stupid enough to write on the backs of our hands / The tingles between my legs when I read certain parts of certain books. What are they? What should I do? / My father exploding, face flushed, eyes bugging out, scaring us to mute submission.

(Trying to) Hay with My Grandmother

They're raking the field for the last time, baling
this afternoon. My grandmother promised she'd be here,
wanted to see it, she'd heard so much about it, just forgot about
her lunch date with Aunt Harriet—lobster for sure—

Harriet finally ate some on her fortieth birthday. Now
she can't get enough of it. It wasn't that it wasn't kosher,
no one keeps kosher, just those red feelers made her squeamish.
By the time she gets back, the bales are already stacked

in the barn. Says she's sorry she missed it, adjusts
the single strand of pearls on her simple black dress. Missed it
again, oh, she's so sorry. Last year it was her literary group—
next year, absolutely. Tomorrow's a long day, first a meeting

with the management, they've fired the Negro doorman—
no reason at all, seems they have a cousin fresh from Ireland—
after that, tea with the illustrator of her children's book
about a small girl who keeps making impossible mistakes, just gets
stupider and stupider. It's killing. Oh, look at your arms, all red and

prickled from the hay. Do you need some Noxzema? Now she's weary,
retires to her bed in the guest room. She'd like a cup of consommé, a little
endive, a dish of toasted almonds, if it's not too much trouble, if someone
could bring it up. She promised us, my brothers and me, a story.
Maybe tomorrow, if she gets some sleep tonight.

Speaking with My Mother

At sixteen my mother has a raging infection.
They operate, remove her mastoid bone,
leave a cavern behind her ear, so deep
she's written up in medical journals.
With her head still swathed in bandages
she swims across Jordan Lake—
a small lake but still—
to impress a boy she's sweet on, a sandy-haired
boy, son of the caretakers at her family's summer place.
When I am a child she tells me I can explore that cave—
I put my finger inside, roam its darkness, its ridged, repellant
seduction—
long to shrink, small enough
to curl up inside.
Don't talk to me on my left side, she says,
I can't hear you.

My mother cannot hear me speak,
asks me the same question
over and over
nods, pretends, asks again
the next day and the day after.
I speak slowly,
clearly. It doesn't help.
She lets fly cruel words
Do you get along with anybody?
sends them soaring through the space between us.
Don't talk to me.
Sometimes, when I allow myself
I remember being her small, sweet daughter
stand-in for her own fledgling self
the one who swam the lake to prove herself, a white bandage
wrapping the hole behind her ear.

Green Gloves

My mother says:
I don't remember who gave me these,
drops a pair of kid gloves
into a circus of silk scarves, the chaos of

her bureau drawer. Again I am fourteen
in Florence on the Ponte Vecchio, missing
home. August heat blisters on ochre walls.
I choose a gift for my mother—
oasis refreshment, sherbet palette,

mint green. She says:
I don't remember who gave me these.
I've always hated them.
Suddenly, I am a doe, leading the hunter
away from my fawn.
I will not tell her it was me.

Spanish Civil War: My Father's Choice

—after Irena Klepfisz

Because he believed in democracy
Because he flirted with communism
Because he hated Franco
Because he wanted to be a hero
Because his father told him not to
Because he wanted to make a difference and this seemed
like his chance
Because he hoped to be brave

Because he didn't like guns
Because he had to finish law school
Because he didn't like trenches
Because he had other things to do
Because his father told him not to
Because he'd just met a woman
Because the guy who headed his cell told him he was
staying behind to recruit more men
and he didn't believe him
Because he was afraid
to say he was scared

Music Box

                    Dinners my father yelled
then he'd storm down the cellar stairs   did he know
to his amber screwdrivers, his glockenspiel   the power of
of wrenches, his rasps, his files   his peeled green eyes
his planes, his nails and screws   naked as fish
his contrapuntal hands that all day pounded   his red face like
typewriter keys   an overblown balloon
now patiently ministering   the barrage of his
to an old chest of drawers   machine-gun voice—
stripping paint, unearthing   we'd stare
wood-grain, laying down   at our plates
new satin skin.   trying to
The winter he bought   disappear
26 music box movements he was   bow our heads
down there every night   as if before god
building them wooden boxes   never saw
painting them crayon colors, each box   the frightened wizard
with a square of glass so you could   hidden behind the curtain
see the polished drum, the fine brass keys   the small man
arched back, sprung free. Then he began   scared
his magnum opus, a perfect model   of his power tools
of our house, crept Dutch eaves, measured   his wife's money
windows, roof slope, scoured   his own rage
hobby shops for tiny pines, yew   holed up down there
pachysandra. Unveiling day   in the basement
he wound the key, released   putting his explosive love
the tiny instrumentalist inside   into a magnificent music
            sweetly plinking HomeSweetHome

Polish Guide

In Krakow I hire a guide, a man a little younger than my father.
   He picks me up in his decrepit car,
drives me to Auschwitz, asks on the way did I have family here—
   In Poland, yes, I tell him,
a shtetl two hours southeast of Krakow, not in the camps, thank
   god, they left fifty years before the war.
We pass through the gates, their ringing greeting—
   Artbeit Macht Frei—I follow him as we tour the barracks,
endless rows of identical red brick, dead ivy clinging
   to the walls. He chooses our route, first the exhibits of
Polish heroism, Polish loss—stops before each panel,
   makes sure I read each line, then buildings with
the other exhibits, Jews and Gypsies, wall after wall of
   paired head shots, front view, side view—has little to say—
mountains of shoes suitcases with their owners' names
   prayer shawls toothbrushes human hair bleached
of all color—me, glutted numb—then more Polish exhibits,
   always hissing in my ear—trapped, his story, his pain,
his father in the underground, caught, imprisoned here at
   Auschwitz (lucky for him he survived)—I am
cornered as with my father, learn of the millions of Polish
   dead—the barrage of my father's thoughts, my father's
feelings—and I am guilty, hadn't known, and I won't look
   at my guide—though I need to know—as I wouldn't look
at my father—try not to let his words insinuate themselves
   in my ear, his weighing of bodies—
dead Poles on this scale, dead Jews on that—hear again
   my father's words:
      What do you have to complain about?

Not That It's So Much Easier

For me, being a Jew among Jews—Fridays I stand at the
intersection dressed in black holding a sign END THE
OCCUPATION protesting what Israel does in our names—razing
olive groves, bulldozing homes, annexing land that was given to
others.

In Israel, Women in Black get cursed, pelted with garbage. Here
in Canada they're more polite. Still, we know what they say behind
our backs: *Traitors, Finishing what Hitler started.*

Then going home to light the candles.
There wasn't much Jewish when I was a child, still
a few words lodged—

You shall not oppress the stranger
(remember we were strangers)
When strangers reside with you, you shall not wrong them
(we were slaves in Egypt)
or the orphan or the widow
(remember how we left, how we roamed the desert)
You shall teach your children

Growing up I never heard a blessing.

At home a huge Christmas tree took up most of the living room,
so tall it scraped the ceiling, a six-pointed tinfoil star on top, hung
with glass ornaments hand-blown in Germany—they'd been in
my mother's family for generations. My parents were easier with
the enormous Christmas tree than the Hanukkah menorah on
the mantle.

I knew what it was to be assimilated.
It took a long time to learn to be Jewish.

Reading Sholom Aleichem Irena Klepfisz Kadia Molodowsky
Primo Levi Abraham Joshua Heschel Martin Buber. Very Jewish
to learn from the pages of books.

Visiting synagogues and cemeteries: Bombay Hong Kong Rangoon
New Delhi Prague Budapest Morocco Mexico City New Orleans
Alabama Mississippi Paris Rome Kensington Market the Lower
East Side . . .

Every year at Pesach my father read these words
    from the Hagaddah:
You Shall not Oppress the Stranger
Words that held me, touched me in a way I didn't
    understand.

I felt I was the stranger, never Jewish enough among Jews, no
religious training, knowing no Hebrew, imitating the cantor's
SHEMA YISRAEL in the carpool home from Sunday school, his
high-pitched wail, words we didn't know, no one explained. Bereft
of culture, knowing just the few Yiddish words my parents used,
the same ones radio hosts love—*schmooze schmatte schlemiel.*

Still, I was a Jew. Wherever I went they knew me. In Florence at
fourteen a man knocked on the car window, gave us directions to
the synagogue. In Merida a French tourist picked me out. Kayaking
off Vancouver Island a woman from Michigan found me.

You know the feelings of the stranger

Me, always the stranger, too Jewish for the rest of the world, trying
to buy Passover matzohs in my local supermarket: *Oh, you mean
maz-toes, no, we don't have them.*

Looking for secret Jews in Abiquiu, descendants of *anousim* who followed Columbus. Searching for scattered Jews in tiny pastel *shuls* south of Bombay. A derelict synagogue in Memphis, now a derelict jazz club, a star of David above the cracked neon. In small towns across Oklahoma, Arizona, a hot springs resort in Arkansas.

Learning to find the old Jewish businesses in small towns across the American South, traces of Jewish merchants, middlemen to rural planters—classic brick buildings, names emblazoned on the fronts, small towns, bigger cities . . . the Jews long gone.

Remember we were strangers . . .

Unseen, misunderstood. Startled by offensive comments no one else thought twice about: The auctioneer at the farmers' market selling a lot of calves, when the bidding got slow: *Oh, the Jews from Sooke are here.* The old lady across the street, a woman I loved—every Sunday she dressed in her Salvation Army uniform, went off to church. When I told her I was Jewish: *You didn't have to tell me that, Dear. You must be good with money, Dear.*

Now Tuesday evenings I study Hebrew, learn to read the letters, right to left, sing the blessing over the candles, Friday mornings I braid challah, prepare for Shabbat . . .

Maybe because my father read:
And you shall teach your children

Though how much, he wasn't sure—certainly not the old customs his parents had abandoned: the *seders* at his grandparents', the long table stretching the length of the flat, his grandfather reading every prayer, his uncles begging him to hurry, my father with the other kids under the table, giddy on homemade wine. My family's seders were tiny and dignified, no relatives, no chaos—

and no singing. We were the latest in a long story: shrimp cocktail at my Brooklyn grandmother's, sailing on Rosh Hashanah, eating our way through Yom Kippur. My mother remembered only one childhood *seder* at some relative's, her embarrassment when she asked for butter at a meat meal, stuffing too-hot horseradish into her bloomers—it left a purple stain.

The sword comes into the world because of
justice delayed

Never again, we say, meaning different things:
Never again to Us, or Never again to Anyone.

You shall welcome the stranger and those who
are in need

As I do, welcoming Jewish strays, those whose families never observed, those who've just found a Jewish grandmother in Denmark, a father whose father was a Cohen in Scotland . . .

Because I know what it is to be shamed
for not knowing, shamed for being . . .

the wrongly imprisoned, the beggar in the street

Waiting eagerly for Pesach, the table laden with food, long evenings with friends telling stories, creating our own ways to be Jewish, making space for love and grief and . . .

The widow and the orphan

Bite of beet-red horseradish

Together they shall be . . .

Tang of apples walnuts sweet wine

Let all who are hungry . . .

Reminding me to set the table, put out the candles,
my *seder* plate from a Palestinian pottery in East Jerusalem.
Come and eat . . .

Olives, dates, pomegranates
gefilte fish, *kugel*
golden soup flecked with *schmaltz*

And I will bring you into the land . . .

Jerusalem, next year

I open the door for Elijah

I, may I find home

—after Yehuda Amichai

I, may I find home. I have lived too long
in echoing rooms, darkness
making more darkness, too long between brocade
and squalor, an undeclared war
where bridges are targets and difference
a cudgel, too long amid shredded garments.
I want a coat knit just for me
from family yarn. I will cobble a basket
from forgotten prayers, lost recipes, walk
through the razed city, gathering
silenced language, forbidden laps. I will climb no ladders,
only rest in the chant of gift-giving tongues,
build a house for my fellows, a generous house,
set the table, places for my ghosts
and time to listen. I will bind myself to mystery,
its flow from narrowed walls into opening.
Let me come home.

3

Love allows us to walk
in the sweet music of our particular heart.

—Jack Gilbert

Ruach

three swallows skim the field, arcing
dipping

weaving the world: warp
of wild oats and daisies, weft
spun of light

breath   wind   spirit

three swallows
is a world

two crows caw by
and the sum is five

a hawk riding the updraft
makes six, soaring, circling
for a vole
hiding in deep grass, seven

seven gods:

let seven stand for uncountable riches
one   seven   infinitude

eight is me witnessing

all held
in a wheeling
stillness

Mountains and Poetry—Banff, 2003

The blue mountains are constantly walking.
If you doubt mountains walking,
you do not know your own walking.
                                    —Dogen

Poetry reading, outside the window pin-up mountains,
Canada's best, ragged jagged upright stones.
The poet called them with her dark chocolate voice.
They heard, drew imperceptibly closer.
How can I tell you of my ravishment—
one eye on the poet, the other on the peaks.
Nothing between us but thin glass. I looked again,
obliquely. Mountains are shy. I had no wish to offend
their privacy. But when, against all judgment I stared,
they balked. Behind the white peaks, big-bellied clouds,
bottoms with the blush of a July peach, scudding,
streams of them, moving fast. Below, paintbrush pines
swayed green on pencil trunks—together/apart/together/
apart, like lovers. The mountains withdrew leaving a pale
parody of themselves and the finest gold strand
edging their form so that I could, with kindergarten
care cut along the line, pull them from the sky.

Saskatchewan Tikkun

It's easy to learn the things you love
                    —Trevor Herriot

All week it's snowed another kind
of snow—poplar fluff gently swirling, wind-carried,
speckling the clarion blue of the sky
and the leaves of the caragana still
silvered with newness. Wolf willow
wakes me with its
funky fragrance. The world tugs at
my sleeve, calls me from my rootless
way as chicks, all down and beak, call to their parents:

> Here.
>   Hear.

And I listen, try to learn
willow's breath, the tongues
of grass: brome rush sedge. I want to know
the voice of sod, talk with it of loss,
restoration. Begin the repair. Hey, Crow,
teach me
your names.

Ora et Labora

Double file pines, green-black ranks
planted one hundred years ago in grids

like the roads. They ring the abbey, an act
of faith—green spires rising from prairie flat.

More than windbreak, they are boundary.

Inside the pines an open palm,
wide beds for rows of spinach
carrots, potatoes, beans.

Lunch time. Abbey produce. Under their robes the monks
just in from the fields, wear Levi's and work boots.

Brother Thomas takes the stairs two at a time
Whistling *O Canada*, his stride fanning his black skirt.

This morning he sharpened hoes, oiled blades,
hung each tool back in its outline on the wall.

After lunch Brother Andrew will mow between stones
in the graveyard, tucked inside an evergreen circle
down an evergreen alley. Where they will lie.

Brother Basil will prune apple trees, water shoots that scrape the sky,
tame them into soft rounds. Work and worship, precise rhythm.
Until the bell for vespers.

A pulse. In the abbey lawn a ragged prairie rose.
The monks clip the grass just up to it, leave the weeds.

In the Brush by the Railroad Tracks or the Gully by the Stream

Beyond the monks' care, this
humming machine

their precisely industrious abbey
you can tune to rhythms still barely there

beneath the grid of county roads and fields:

wind through native grass and sod
deer springboard
mouse temple, buffalo run once, and

home to the people who
followed them

their last notations
weathered tent rings

circles of rocks
mostly gone.

By day you might find butter yellow
ladyslippers, in the gully
tway-blade

and at night
lightning bugs
a Las Vegas of blinking stars—

handkerchiefs of fallow
overlooked, forgotten, falling away.

Danceland Saturday Night

The parking lot is full when they get there.
The Decades on stage, beetle blue shirts
slicked back hair.
They've danced here forty years
missed a few—
      seeding and harvest, otherwise
               like clockwork.

                  His hand on her elbow,
he guides her to the skating rink
of a floor, a little unsure
except when they dance.
He pulls her in, steadies himself.
      The room breathes—fast to a polka,
                  slow
                     to a waltz.
Elvis is their home, easy listening
the way this band plays
"Moon River". Her flowered skirt swings wide
     dandelions under prairie breeze.
          Summer evenings stretch
              and stretch
                like fields of canola.

No rain this year, seed prices sky high, elevators going
or gone—and the farm debt.

Red paper lanterns warm the dusk,
    the mirrored globe scatters rhinestones
        on their shoulders and the floor.

Friends chat of kids, away in the city, maybe
for a while, mostly
        for good.

The couples on the floor another kind of
family, Saturday night
          constellations, moving round
                    and round, holding their ground.

Tomato Fugue

This is not tomato country, our nights
too cold for their red blood.
In a good year, tomatoes rise on a scarlet tide
but not till the cicadas cry. Other years
blight cuts them down.
I load bushels with brown-pocked fruit,
tumbrel them to distant burial

and remember Aunt Libby, alone in the old house,
her cherry table seated twelve, too large
for Libby and the neighbor woman who helped out.

In her September garden, below the clothes line
beside the woodshed, the last tomatoes sprawled—
grown from seed her daughter sent
from Italy, Mama Pelagatti's *pomodoro* seed,

tomatoes to coddle and sauce noon's pasta,
a name for every shape:
semi di mela, farfalle, creste di gall —
apple seeds, butterflies, cockscombs.

In the star-crisp twilight Aunt Libby ran
from cupboard to cupboard, gathered armloads
of blankets, swaddling for her *pomodori*,
tucked them in against fall's dark chill.

*

Tomatoes are ripened ovaries, lush
promise of generation. This year
my moons have cooled, my body now
dry riverbed, wind-washed canyon.

I find myself weeping for children
I might have had.

*

In a season of dissolution
in the poignance of October's blue perfection
I prune tomato plants, cut away their leaves,
leave only stems, skeleton structure,
distract myself from my own story

till I am called to a liquid purring, sweet intimacies,
and above, four eagles, soaring
this dry land where no salmon run, circling
the stretched-canvas sky.

I pick up my pruners again
expose late fruit to light's last stream.

Calling

I am calling you back
    as a ewe
        baas to her lambs
    as the pigeon man
        whistles his doves

trying to remember how I did it before, offering
touchstones
    the quail
        a whole family in the brush pile
    spring's slow snakes
        their yellow-green stripes

reminding you
    what you love
    the dog
        head raised watching crows crossing clouds
    the bats
        patrolling the pond for bugs
    the porcelain
        of a pullet's first eggs
    the candle in its tin-can sconce
               the Guatemalan cloth
    our bodies
        nested, two halves of a walnut

calling you back
    to yourself

    to me

Southern mist and the ecumenical world is singing

For the place on which you stand—it is holy ground!
                    —Exodus 3:5

Look: see how
sweetgum nestles with oak and loblolly, how

Spanish moss writes linked haiku,
grass script on a sky moist

                    as new-made paper

how the squirrel tucks
into the crotch of the pine where limb meets
trunk

                    holds his hands

in prayer as he eats his acorn
manna
                    how this world all grey

and grey and grey
is singing text

and the curled hands of fallen
leaves
                    verse
                    and response

Zimzum: Creation with Caribou

The river is moving
The blackbird must be flying
                    —Wallace Stevens

In those northern days there was no night, only a
dimming as if the world dozed, then raised

its head. That first day a wind shivered the land,
strong as judgement, so strong you could lie on it. Then

it drew back, stilled—a frieze of pink rock, scrub
willow. That was the second day. On the third day

one solitary scout grazing sedge and cotton grass,
erratic harbinger of the fourth day, knots of animals

moving soft together blurring the horizon, riffling
the sky. The fifth day the land turned liquid, a spate,

horned and furred, one organism with ten thousand
legs, filling the hunger that had been there, the earth's

longing for breath

Haying with Gertrude and Alice

Gertrude sits like a mountain, dark skirt falling
    over her knees, asks me to speak to her of haying:
    blue shadows on new mown stubble
    stripes of felled grass like the field's fingerprint
    straight lines and whorls, the breathless space
    when the bales are gone.
Alice, a smaller mountain in a finer chair, wants
    to speak of scent—how you smell the coumarin
    before you see the shorn field.

Both want to hear how the mules are behaving
two big mollies named for them, Gertrude and Alice
monumental like them and dignified
childless like them, like them paired

want to hear how the reins tangle
whether they stand quiet
    while I load the wagon
    or shift uneasily
    stamping their hooves, one rearing her head
to bite the other's neck
as they do

when they're alone.
Gertrude writes sexual explosion,
cows between the legs, she calls it.
Alice writes of food as climax, culmination—
    their words like pomegranate seed—soft red flesh
    wrapping dark seed. The language of hay

is another seduction:
tedder, harrows, whippletree,
another country, distant
as the world they were born to.

Do they toy with me, my talk of mules?
They do not wish to draw close to hay.
Nothing can shake them
from this rare paradise.

Haying

Let it not rain. Let the wind blow
enough to suck the damp but not
hasten the clouds that bring the rain.

Let swallows wing the field
looping after bugs, let the baler
not break
let field mice scuttle fast from the hawks
but let the hawks
be fed. And the snakes,
may they slide from the baler's maw

let dragonflies zig   hover   zag
neon blue on a cusp of sky.
Now the buzzard hunkers in the stubble. Let him gorge
fast and clean as an executioner's blade.

And let it not

rain. And if it must, let it be
a sprinkle

Let the hayers mop their brows with salty bandanas
let them drink deep—lemon soda, Mexican beer
let the barn fill with hay and the stashed eggs
of renegade hens.

Then, rain

Scar

On the soft stretch of my left arm, the inner arm—just
below the elbow—faint now, the outline of a tooth, the arm
that reached for Sam. He'd been crazy

restless, I let him out to pee, he bolted, searching for
you on the straight stretch of road where Saturday drivers
speed to the sea—me, yelling *SamSamSam*,
seeing it even before it happened—Sam glanced
by one car, hit by another, howling, lurching,
dragging his hind end, sinking by me at the road's edge,
me reaching—
                           we were vacationing,
knew no one, you'd gone to town for bits of hardware to
fix blinds that had crashed when I'd pulled their cord—

cars screeching to stop, strangers offering help.
A vet in town gave him the shot. I held his head wishing I
could be the one he longed for, wishing you were there
to ease him, wishing I'd never
let him out, you hadn't gone to town, I hadn't
broken the blind,
wishing, for a moment, we'd never
let him into our hearts.

In the Throat Mountains

Wind rises before light, whispers Ute Shoshone Paiute
weaves last year's sallowed grass into carrying baskets
for pinyon cones.

And then the sun. Slight as thrush breath.

A narrow trail, feints and switchbacks, takes me—
folds me in nippled sandstone
belly smooth, yellow pink. I rise,

smoke through the hole in the sky. And I am

gauze cloud, ochre rock
purple sage trembling to twig shadow.
Me, the song
in the pinyon pine. Me,
the wind that licks the salt
from my face.

Khirkha, Palestinian woman's veil, silk cross-stitch on handspun linen, Museum for Textiles, Toronto

I cross the gallery, feel my breath catch
seeing these *khirkas* blooming like
walled gardens on the stark white wall, stitched designs
remembered from childhood: a vase of leaves
like an outstretched palm, a bird on a rose, a border
edging the desert of unbleached linen.
It might have been
                    my grandmother
who wove this linen, stitched silk gloss—red, sienna,
burnt umber, like the soil of the Galilee—my
grandmother who worked me a crewel purse,
cerulean, cherry, rose.

           In 1890 her parents filled a wagon
with their kids, their candlesticks, a brass mortar
and pestle, left a Polish *shtetl* for the Lower East Side.
Semitic hands, Semitic cross-stitch.
They might just as well have gone east

                    to Palestine.
Is this appropriation, this blurring of boundaries?
Would they care, those women who made these veils
sixty years ago, their grandchildren now in Nablus,
Hebron, throwing rocks at Israeli tanks that shell
their houses, their schools?

                 Would they care
that I am a weaver, know the grab as the spindle's twist
runs up the thread, the spring of yarn reeling
from the shuttle?

                 I remember Ramallah,
Palestinian women gathering olives
their skirts hiked, scarves pushed back
sun coppering their foreheads.

Forgive me
this lack of separation.
The whole world is a narrow bridge.
For thinking our divisions might be set in softer stone.
The important thing is not to be afraid.
That the lay of bright silk on linen web
could be a bridge
                        that I cross,
hands, feet, heart, into that dusty grove,
look up at the faces of the women in the olive trees,
hold out a basket to receive the fruit.

Challah

When night fills my house
with passages,

I begin saving
my life.

—Marcia Falk

Challah must be made with eggs and blessed
by a rabbi, information I picked up
somewhere, as if I'm some kind of
Jewish expert. My friend's mother takes no notice,
cracks in the eggs, keeps working the sponge,
kneading in flour when it gets sticky.
Friday morning loaves braided from four fat strands
of yellow dough rise on the stove. No rabbi here. Just
one woman, one morning, two hands.
She says she is saving her life.

*

Challah must be made with eggs and blessed
by a rabbi. I make no comment—as if the *shtetl*
rabbis tangled in *pilpul* had time for challah and frantic
Friday women, shopping, scrubbing, plucking—a race
against sundown. Friday mornings I work

this yeasty mystery. Challahs rise like mushrooms to rain.
Eggs from the hens, honey from the bees, seeds
from last summer's poppies. She acts like some kind of

pundit. I am the beginner, cobbling practice from
hearsay and how-to books. Challah on Fridays, candles
dipped for the *hanukkiyah* my father bought in London,
frying latkes so each strand of Yukon Gold crisps.
A practice, if not belief, a way to
reweave fabric, the one I grew up with
frayed, our Jewishness
vestigial. In the city, Jews were everywhere. Here
in the country I found a hunger, found myself
strange fruit, rooting down in alien soil.
Now, Shabbat I light candles, sing

the blessings, dip challah in sweet
wine from the Japanese plums. I fall asleep
almost before dinner ends.

Fawn

Neat as a fur muff curled by the side of the road,
I thought she was sleeping. Days later, the stench
knocked me breathless, pushed me away before it
pulled me back to look, long and slow at her bones,
now a shimmer of slow-moving maggots. Then they were
gone leaving the piano keys of her ribs exposed
as the steps of a chord, and her hair, what was left of it,
curled like fireweed seeds.

When the butcher lived here he did the slaughtering—
calves, lambs, butcher hogs—for the whole
neighborhood, poured the blood over his garden.
Neighbors tell of his peas, big as Brussels sprouts,
his lilies like cabbages. First days of the new year,
night streaks the trees,

clangs the bronze bell in the wisteria, rings out
crumpled wrapping paper, the last of the shortbread,
rings spareness—leeks, turnips, beet greens.
Nights like this the gusting wind is the bell's pulse.
No grass yet. Sheep stand on hind legs, nibble
fir bark. Alder sap and maple, already rising, already
the witch hazel flames, first of all blooms,
fine fingers clenched, then lets go. Along the road
wind plays the fawn's bones, her hair felted now after
a season under snow. Soon nothing

will hold her. I will gather her bones, light now
and white, gather them in my arms, gather
her shiny black hooves, string them
into clackers, rhythm for my song.

Sunday Afternoon and Bach is Playing

The eye of the fire, the red turning to ash.
My father puts on another log, my mother
puts on another LP—Wanda Landowska
playing Golberg Variations.
                              In this always winter
music knits me into afternoon, the dark drawing in
early, a cave with a black stone hearth, the tick
of the clock, its chimes. I burnish the coat
of the Irish Setter, lay my head
                              in the hollow
where her leg meets her belly, safety thick as
barley soup, buttered toast, the rug awash
in the New York Times, discarded sections scattered
like leaves.
                    My mother reads the theater section,
my father works the double-crostic. Later we will
send out for Chinese food in white cardboard cartons
with metal handles

                    and I never want to leave this room,
where music curtains darkening glass, carpets the floor,
cushions my head.

There is a Moss

called Resurrection Plant, dead grey
without water, in rain it rears up

bright and new. This is the Arizona desert
just north of the Mexican border. If the burning bush

burnt green it would burn the color of that moss or
these palo verde bushes, smooth polished trunks,

feathery leaves, mellow as old copper. Everything here
is heat and sand, even in winter, but walk

into the hollow of the arroyo—smell the moisture
in green shadows. This desert is shape-shifter, now

a dry and dusty nowhere, now ruined saguaro temple,
ionic columns standing, tilting, fallen, now a sermon,

sharp fingers of desert fathers preaching to the sky.
Haven for perched hawks. Holes where pygmy owls

nest. In one storm these cacti guzzle water, bloat
thorny pleats to swollen rounds, enough water for

one two three seasons. How many greens
in this world of sand?

How many colors is fire?

Let us praise the Garry Oak

Whose bark is braille
Whose leaves, lobed as lungwort, unfold like rusty
    hands

Who are part of the tribe of oak
Who sustain small creatures, whose acorns are hoard for
    stellar jays

Who stretch their limbs in benediction, over camas,
    shooting star, chocolate lily
Who play Capture the Flag, Rule the Roost, King of the
    Mountain

Whose roots hold soil where there is none
Who anchor the sky, beside arbutus and fir

Who know how to wait for water, dapple sunlight

Whose trunks bend to their fellows, whose limbs dance
    Matisse, a circle, a map of the wind's spiral

Who from salty outcrops witness whales: the orcas,
    the greys
Who remember Raven and Snotboy

Whose stomata breathe poetry: Somenos   Songhees
    Sechelt   Tsartlip
Who, like a Japanese courtesan, trail their branches,
    ripple the mirror of the sound

Whose crotches fork the firmament
Who present the sky with a roundness

Who grow lichen like a second skin, the grey scaly kind,
    the pale flat kind

Whose pocked leaves, all marred and mottled, hold on
  despite disfigurement

Who send forth seeds to probe the soil, grow deep, then
  rise again: two leaves, four leaves, a tree

Whose smooth round scars where limbs once grew teach us
  to heal loss
Who play nursemaid to new-hatched crows
Who move their fingers in comfort: There, there . . .
  there, there
Do they conduct the breeze or lean on it?
Whose winter visage is snow on sable

Who persevere though we pave their meadows:
  the mist-hung meadows, the musky meadows, the
  deer-leapt, the wasp-buzzed, the sun-gilt meadows

Who do not come when they're called, who bow but do not
  scrape
Who even fenced in urban yards sing wildness

Who are scrupulous in their ways
Who do not apologize

Who stand their ground
Who let the stars shine through

4

There are mountains hidden in mountains.
There are mountains hidden in hiddenness.

—Dogen

Crossroads Poem

Like deer, drink last night's rain
where it cups in teasel leaves.

Follow geese. They know
to thread the stream, contour
the hills, hold the tissue paper sky.

Watch the blackbird, his narrow
eyebrow of color. When he lifts
he rises to flame.

Do not doubt
the owl's shadow on dark sand, or the
snake as she slides between parsley
green onions and peas.

Even if she steals your breath.
Welcome her.

Remember Snotboy, born of grief.
We are made of dirt and snot
and severed limbs.

Tend your wounds.

Live at crossroads.

Span of Ravens

You think because you understand one you understand two,
Because one and one make two but you must understand and . . .
                —Sufi proverb

                    Neither two
                         nor one
                    yoked
                soaring
                    then tumbling
                         slow-
                                   ly
                         circling down
                a moving center
                    no
                    destination
                    a dyad
                sooty
                    feathers
                    spread
                to break the fall
                    two
                         becoming
                                   other
                    delirium
                barely brushed
                         quills
                                   ec-
                              stasy
                    of *and*

Haying with Groucho

Outside of a dog, a book is man's best friend.
Inside of a dog, it's too dark to read.
                    —Groucho Marx

I make the turn, giving the wagon a wide girth round the hillock.
I'm picking up hay bales scattered in the field—clear June sky,
which is good. I need to get the hay in before it rains—and there's
Groucho, sitting on an old kitchen chair, green paint chipping,
tipping it back against the red bark of the arbutus, a big fat stogey
between his teeth, waggling his eyebrows at me like it's been a
long time and it has. He's a long way from

New York but so am I, him just the age of my grandfather, a
travelling salesman—women's lingerie. Groucho's family were on
the stage, funny guys. My grandfather wasn't funny. *Long way
from a good pastrami sandwich*, he says. I turn off the tractor,
walk over for a closer look. *Thought I could use a break from all
that smoke and smog.* He's coughing a little, unused to clean air.
Then I remember, he's got the same birthday as me, October 2nd—
though he's fifty years older—him, Gandhi, Wallace Stevens and
me,

what a bunch. Tells me his grandparents were smallholders, in
Alsace and Germany. He's heard his parents' stories—a cow, some
geese to fatten, a plot for cabbage, wishes he'd seen them—thought
he'd blow in, see how things were going, says he remembers me
from before, my wild frizz of hair sticking out below my hat, just
like Harpo's, maybe we're related. Maybe we are. I have an Alsatian
grandmother, too.

Heard I've been getting into trouble lately, standing with the radicals, calling for an end to the occupation, the West Bank, that is. *Reminds me of the old days, the FBI after me, commy pinko. Hang in*, he says. I tell him I've got to get the hay in the barn but I'll cook him some matzoh ball soup when I'm done, broth from my own chickens, full of *schmaltz*, or some blintzes, whatever he wants. I climb into the seat, start up the tractor, haul the wagon to the other side of the rise, load another stack of bales. When I come back around, the chair's toppled over and he's gone.

Jew in the Abbey

I have reason to believe we'll all be received . . .
                                        —Paul Simon

These things I know how to receive: the golden-eyed
peonies in the abbey garden, the long-tailed magpies

Chasing a bone-thin mama cat, even the bloodsucker ticks
waving come-on arms from dry grass. And the voices.

There is always song in the abbey. The monks face each
other across two banks of desks, alternate verses,

left side, then right side, their voices resonating
through the empty space of the silver girders.

The abbey welcomes us all. When I lose my place
in the songs a brother is there at my elbow, showing me

the way. Angels of all sorts in the abbey. In my room I
contemplate the promise sung this morning at lauds, to

protect Abraham and his Children forever. Outside,
a monk in a baseball cap and striped overalls rides his

red mower, cutting grass already cut, sending up
a wake of green shards. Like fireflies. A bell rings

and rings. Rings again. Calling monks to vespers.
Calling me. They sing the cycle of Psalms,

Old Testament words, Father Son and Spirit tacked on
the end. Is this welcome, this building on the body

of my people's book, as the conquistadors built churches
over Inca temples they'd destroyed? The monks' song

carries me. Can I receive as well the three
kinds of bread from the abbey kitchen, the turning

from the world to build this world, an acceptance of

a mystery that will never be mine, the glide past
the monastery silo, the silence of owl flight?

Honey House

The air in the honey house is waxy smooth and thick
like breathing under water. Father Demetrius flaps
the scapular on his black cassock, shoos flies.
Does his chest thicken in the still sweet air?

Below his skirt an edge of denim work pants, his robes
for worship, vespers and lauds. He shows us the stack
of supers, empty combs, hexagonal cells, honey
extracted now. Takes us to the clearing in the poplars

where fourteen beehives hunker. He keeps the grass
around them cropped, respect for his children—that's
what he calls them. He won't go closer now.
Bees don't like black. Or wind. Or overcast days but

when the sun's out they beeline south to the canola,
east to the raspberries, west to the apple trees.
He shows us the old green tractor he uses to haul the hives,
the one Brother Xavier used, called it his

baby—he can still hear Xavier chiding him if he
throttles too fast, the monks mostly older now, only
a few young ones. Some come, few stay. He tells us
how he raises queens, his recipe for mead, how he

heats the combs, puts them in the extractor, spins out
the honey—a miracle, pollen into gold, another
kind of prayer.

I will ask for birds

—Kelly Parsons

I have asked for birds.
Scanned tree tops, listened for owls
come up blank, my consolation
    the corrugated silos struck silver in first light,
the rainwash smell of damp earth
    harrowed round.

The morning Brother Anthony surprised me
    with his blessing
I walked again, looking
    without hunger this time. Till I heard a sigh
in the wild cherries
    where the tree's shadow unfolded
        a preening form, head hidden inside dusky wing.
        It raised its eyes, locked gaze with mine.

        Great Horned Owl   so close

I faltered, it lifted
    leading me into the eyes of a chick
        the down on its breast. It startled, rose
    and I was staring into
        the open beak of a second
            like a string of silent firecrackers
                each one igniting the next and me
        frozen in the raw pull of wild gaze
        the tree split
        three hearts six eyes
        allowing me
            the crack in the door
            the thinnest slice of that other world
              held in the terror of wonder
            till the last chick
                flew to a darker grove.

Haying with Murasaki Shikibu

Lady Murasaki knows the etiquette of hay—
    the proper paper for the note to the bailer—rusty red
        like arbutus bark—tied with a darker cord the color
        of its berries,
    what the hayers should wear—*haori,* the deep blue
        of the June sky, pale blue *hakama* the color of dawn,
    the order of the procession: the master leading the mules,
    then seven scythers, six tedders with their polished
    pitchforks, one lone singer.

Murasaki will sit in the gallery with the other ladies
    behind bamboo screens, refresh herself
        with a lacquered fan, note this man's noble bearing,
        that man's perfect ass,
    the gall of the lead horseman, sending his snot
    flying from his nostrils.

The notes of a *shakuhachi* rest on the air like oil
    on water.

Down the road, I hitch up my overalls—the shoulder strap
that slides to my elbow—haul myself onto the tractor,
get the damn thing going. Two fields still to ted—
Dale hates to wait supper—pop a plug of tobacco into
my mouth, hork the juice

all thought killed in the clank and jangle of the machine.

In the evening Murasaki grinds sumi on her black
inkstone, dips her brush, commits her musings to a sheet
of *gampi,* translucent as sun's last light, slides the paper
beneath her pillow.

I hobble in, innards jounced from hours
on the metal seat,
fill the old iron tub, pour epsom salts,
soak my feet.

Boxing Day Field

You must stand still to see the robins in the stubble
everywhere, a hidden host, only the round of their heads
betraying a shared intelligence
in the scrabble of dry bracken and pigeon
grass, their eyes, a darker constellation.

You must
allow this twilight to crack you. Breathe
the frost. Now raise your arms,

watch the field unfurl its curtain of wings.

We need
the robins' dreaming to remind us of
our intricacies, the breadth of this narrow ledge

we inhabit
between the lichen and the elk
the earthworm and the bristle-cone pine.

Burning Bush

When you walk across the fields with your mind
pure and holy, then from all the stones, and all
growing things, and all animals, the sparks of
their soul come out and cling to you, and then
they are purified and become a holy fire in you.
                              —Hasidic saying

Rusty crows rise in a flap of needing
some way to mark the new day,
flash their feathers, watch
for the sun to blush the dry and
empty land. You could yell
and yell and

no one would hear.
Up ahead, sap rising, a bush
flames its naked stalks winter red,
and there another:
signal fires—molten energy

on bare hills.
Is this what Moses saw,
a bush igniting the earth's
incandescent heart,
burned but not consumed?
Was this what he heard—
a silence in the roar
speaking to him
of god?

Barred Owl

Who cooks for you is out tonight writing the sky
with invisible ink, his *moktok* call
    carving itself in velvet, resonant as raven's
      drum, a night
         river, arcing into my bones.

              Who has seen
his shadow cross the hayfield? And still not seen
his feathers, his talons, the rabbit
clenched? By day I find

his lime scrawl on trees, his spit-up pellets, catalogue
    vole skulls, the hip sockets of meadow mice. His call

is a dare. Nights, I wake
to the hollow of his voice, as if he lived
    in the cavity of my chest, teaching me the underside
         of breath. They say he cries out

death. I say he calls me
    to water. I lace
    grass slippers, my straw cape. I want to hear

stars buzz green, blue, the coolest
white, smell the dew
as it falls, sign with arbutus.

         Who cooks for you.
     He hoots, twice.

Silence.
   Then again.

    Who cooks for you.

     I glide to the pitch of the owl's song
     drinking.

The blossoms are so brave

I: Japanese Plum

prescience of fruit, draping bare branches with
pink stars. Early April hardly warmer
than March, frost arranges grass in glittering
swords. There are no guarantees.
Foolhardy blossoms offer haiku
petals to rain-driven bees.
                              Don't speak
of promises unfulfilled. Suspend fear.
Attend beauty.

II: Wild cherry

somersaulting, out of bounds, painting the trees
in white-face
                    rollicking clowns,
cotton candy for swallows, conjuring
joy to a sky serving spring.

III: Quince

perfect rosebuds, torqued petals
engorged
          blushing
                    swelling
                              milk goddesses loosening
wombs—Jung might have dreamt them.

Quince blossoms birth the world.

Goldstream Reprise

                         Like the salmon
I return to Goldstream each fall, drawn to this elbow
of river, this naked
death, salmon
                    eyeless in the shallows
the stench of rotting flesh.

               Above, gulls lace a jagged seam of sky
crisscross between canyon walls
as if to stanch the bloody gash—

                         the dying god
dying into offering: first seed
then flesh for gulls, eagles, bears, food for cedars and fir.

I who can't name home
watch gulls strip skin from hollowed ribcage
temples. In spring, unseen

                    new smolt will slip through the bones
swim dark arteries to siren deeps
until they are called
          home, the taste of the river
                    the contour of
                         the only hills there are.

The Narrow Place

again I am in the narrow place, salt-laced, dry
as a rat long dead in the silverware drawer

at dusk, the lightest drenching of rain
morning the land cracks open

I did not want this spring, willed sap
not to rise in my veins, magnolias to stay locked
in their dun cocoons, preferred

interment, the grey chamois
of my time below ground

it doesn't matter what I want

spring's ferocious magnet
calls song from sleeping froglets
poplars to flush their tiny green blades
bless us with their sweet balm

Pruning Wisteria

My father on the ladder, clipping
chaos, shoots gone wild.
On the ground below a green
morgue, prunings that aimed
to twine the chimney, festoon the garage.
No wonder I've let my wisteria run, let shoots

scrawl curlicues on sky's blank book,
left laterals to tangle with apple,
dried pods to hang like withered scrota.

My father, demon pruner, tried to shape
his children, when he couldn't govern
the panic within.

Wisteria cracks through
asphalt, pulls down roofs.
Reluctantly I climb the ladder, struggle to sort
the tangle, prune deadwood, leave
fat buds bursting to bloom.

When time was food

and night a two hour watch feeding my infant daughter
pumping breast milk heating it holding her by me
while she fattened I slimmed slipping into sleep waking
to her hungry cries when time was food seeding the
still chill soil spring sowing waiting for crops to swell
days to stretch a round stillness nothing to do but pick
peas shell them out rest against sun-warmed walls
storing heat to carry me through winter's dark when
time was food we headed to the scrub for wild blue-
berries indigo seed pearls blushed rose cached in the
low green of the bushes scads of them scooting on our
asses clump to clump kids picking too sometimes there
were bear a mama her cubs we'd creep back give her
space enough for everyone filling the ice cream bucket
feeling fall in the first new snow on the hills three pies
jars and jars of jam on the shelves living along the creek
its milk jade flood that left us sparkly with mica when it
receded husband gone so much his place silted in with
our clothes and books by the time he got home

Blessing

Shehehyanu vikiemanu vehigianu lazman hazeh:
Who has brought us to this season

So we wake:
tongues to new peas
ears to spring peepers

hearts to swallows
home again to waiting nests.

This evening I put a pot to boil,
go out to gather corn.
The garden lies wasted, a few

cukes on a broken frame,
zucchini limp from night's cold breath,

the last of the corn, stunted ears, kernels
gapped but so sweet.
We need another blessing

for last wild cherries,
the sun's stain
on a loon black lake,
the final throb of a small brass bell:

Let us bless the source of life

who shepherds us into the dying away,
abides with us in the moment after.

Haying with Death

We know the image

bones bound
by nothing, black monk's
robes, a scythe with blade
honed, the momentum
of its weight slicing through
too soft flesh.

I like to think of harvest as fruition, not this
dead end.

I have counted death—ducklings
swamped in the water trough, the
too many puppies freighted with rocks
sunk in the river, fairy lambs
too weak to suck, piglets suffocated
beneath their mother's girth, my brother
dead too soon
of an old man's disease, friendships gone,
love failed, the loss of solid ground.

I do not want to live forever, do not
want this body when strength and spirit
go. I will not hang on. Let me
harvest now, whatever love
I can gather to myself, then the parting.
Let those behind sing my bones
reflesh me with memories—
what I gave, what I took.

How Does the Heart

open? Like a walnut
hairline crack in its green fortress

and the armor
             falls away?

             Like the sea, rolling over
drawing back, rearing up
taut Hokusai wave uncurling

into a gentle hand
             of foam?

             Like a head of ripened wheat
bent to the ground
each hard kernel yielding
to the earth's sweet damp

sending soft green shoots
                    from each germ?

                    Like me
             next to you
all these years—
comfort I've struggled to receive

wrapping me now
             in home's cloak

Notes on the Text

p. 9. *Mitzrayim*: Hebrew for Egypt, meaning "narrow places". *Mitzrayim* denotes all kinds of constricted places—the physical desert where water is limited, or our own inner narrowness, the pharaoh within.

p. 16. Tokeiji: a Buddhist temple at Kamakura that provided sanctuary, divorce and refuge, for ill-treated wives.

p. 20. *shtetl*: Yiddish for a small Jewish community in Eastern Europe where Yiddish culture flourished. These were obliterated by the end of World War II.

p. 34. M.O.T.: Members of Our Tribe, code for educated Jews.

kishke: stuffed intestines, the Jewish version of haggis, never eaten in my house.

NAACP: National Association for the Advancement of Colored People.

p. 35. This is the voice of my great grandmother, Evelyn Ehrich, who was, in fact, the first Jew to live at the Dakota, an elegant New York apartment building at 1 West 72nd Street and Central Park West where, about fifty years later, John Lennon was shot as he was returning home on December 8, 1980.

p. 38. *chang*: Tibetan for rice wine.

p. 46. *Anousim:* Jews who fled Spain during the Inquisition, maintained Jewish observance in secret.

Mirame attento, soy tu alimento: Words on a Salamancan bread stamp.

p. 47. Hannah Senesh (1921- 1944), poet, born in Budapest to an assimilated family, emigrated to Palestine, studied agriculture, worked for the Haganah (the Jewish underground), parachuted behind Nazi lines into Yugoslavia, crossed the border into Hungary to work with the partisans hoping to free Jews in the concentration camps. She was captured, tortured to reveal information (she never did) and killed by a firing squad.

Kristallnacht, the Night of Breaking Glass, November 9, 1938, when 191 German synagogues were set on fire.

p. 52. *Goyische*: Yiddish for non-Jewish.

schnecken: sweet rolls shaped like snails.

p. 66. *Arbeit Macht Frei*: sign in German at the entrance to Auschwitz, Work Will Make You Free.

p. 67. The original Women in Black are groups of women, Jewish Israelis and Palestinian Israelis, who stand once a week, dressed in black, in a silent vigil holding signs calling for an end to the Israeli occupation of the West Bank and Gaza. The groups began in Jerusalem and Tel Aviv in 1988 in response to the first Intifada. Groups of women (and sometimes men) in cities around the world hold silent vigils in solidarity with the women of the Middle East. The idea has also spread to other parts of the world where women hold vigil for issues arising in their own locality.

pp. 68-71. *Hagaddah*: text read at the Passover or Pesach *seder*. The word "*seder*" means "order". The word "hagaddah" means "the telling". The hagaddah tells the story of Moses and the Pharaoh, the plagues, and the crossing of the Sea of Reeds (the Red Sea), tells us when to say each blessing and taste each symbolic food—wine, matzoh, bitter herbs, etc. The haggadah's text is ever evolving. Some have been written by women for women's *seders*, some to address Black people's struggle for justice, some center around the conflict in the Middle East. Pesach is primarily a home ritual; no rabbi is needed. This is one way Jews have been able to maintain our customs even while scattered in tiny pockets around the world. All we've needed was memory and one or two other Jews.

Elijah: the prophet of peace. We always place a glass of wine on the *seder* table for Elijah. At a certain point in the *seder*, we open the door to welcome him. In women's *seders* there is also a cup for Miriam, Moses' sister, who led the Jews in singing and dancing after they crossed the Sea of Reeds.

shul: yiddish for synagogue.

p. 75. *ruach*: Hebrew for breath, wind, spirit.

p. 77. *tikkun*: Hebrew for repair, often used in the phrase *tikkun olam*, the repair of the world.

p. 86. *zimzum*: Hebrew for the withdrawal of god from primal space preceding the creation.

p. 93. *Kol ha'olam kulo gesher tsarme'od. Veha'ekar lo lehifached.*

The whole world is a narrow bridge. The important thing is not to be afraid.—Reb Nachman of Bratslav.

p. 94. *pilpul*: Yiddish for techniques of scholarly disputation.

p. 105. Groucho Marx, (1890-1977) born Julius Henry Marx, in New York, son of Sam and Minnie.

Alexander Feingold, (1887-1974), my grandfather, born in the Ukraine, son of Sam and Hannah who immigrated to New York in 1888. The Alsatian grandmother was on the other side.

p. 111. Murasaki Shikibu (c. 976 - 1015) author of The Tale of Genji, a masterpiece of Japanese prose narrative, possibly the earliest true novel in the history of the world.

Acknowledgments

Some of these poems have been published previously, some in different forms, in the following journals: The Antigonish Review, CV2, The Fiddlehead, Grain, The Malahat Review, Parchment, Room of One's Own, Wascana Review, and Xerography. Several have also appeared in *Listening with the Ear of the Heart: Writers at St. Peter's,* the anthology honoring the 100th anniversary of St. Peter's Abbey as a Benedictine monastery in Canada.

I am most grateful to Mary Ann Sampson of OEOCO Press who published *Then From All the Stones*, a limited letterpress edition that included many of these poems. After setting all the lines by hand, she knew my poetry better than I did.

Much appreciation for time spent at the Banff Centre, Sage Hill Writing Experience, and St. Peter's College where a number of these poems were written.

My deepest gratitude to Don McKay for mentoring above and beyond the call of duty

Many thanks to Betsy Warland, Patricia Young, and Patrick Lane, all of whom provided inspiration and guidance when I barely knew if what I was writing was poetry.

I am grateful to Barbara Colebrook Peace, Kelly Parsons, and Susan Stenson, the original members of my writing group that continues, in an expanded form, to be a source of rich ferment and sensitive support.

Many thanks to Oolichan Books, especially to Hiro Boga for her thoughtful editing.

To Rudy, again, love and thanks for listening these many years, and to Cicely, my steady companion this last while.

About the Author

Dorothy Field is a visual artist who has worked with handmade paper for sculpture, prints, and one-of-a-kind books for the last twenty-five years. She began writing poetry during trips to Asia, where she was researching textiles, handmade paper, and scattered Jewish communities. Born in New York, she has lived and farmed on Vancouver Island for more than thirty years.